Feelings
NOTES

Canadian representatives: General Publishing Co., Ltd., 30 Lesmill Road,
Don Mills, Ontario M3B 2T6.

9   8   7   6   5   4   3   2   1
Digit on the right indicates the number of this printing.

ISBN 1–56138–644–8

Cover design by Toby Schmidt
Interior design by Susan E. Van Horn
Edited by Tara Ann McFadden
Printed in the United States

This book may be ordered by mail from the publisher.
Please add $1.00 for postage and handling.
But try your bookstore first!

Running Press Book Publishers
125 South Twenty-second Street
Philadelphia, Pennsylvania 19103–4399

Feelings
NOTES

RUNNING PRESS
PHILADELPHIA · LONDON

*L*ife is like music; it must be composed
by ear, feeling, and instinct, not by rule.

Samuel Butler (1612–1680)
English poet

Feelings are not regular or consistent.
They are all given to us at once, all the
feelings we are ever to experience; like
the flames of a torch, they are squeezed
into our breast from birth.

MARINA TSVETAYEVA (1892–1941)
RUSSIAN WRITER AND POET

Man was a feeling creature long before he was a thinking creature.
The mind is younger than the body and younger than the emotions.

Howard Thurman (1900–1981)
American cleric

Our feelings, like the artist's paints
and brush, are ways of communicating
and sharing something meaningful
from us to the world.

Rollo May (1909–1994)
American psychoanalyst and writer

Our feelings are our most genuine paths to knowledge.

AUDRE LORDE (B. 1934)
WEST INDIAN EDUCATOR, POET, AND WRITER

Seeing is believing, but feeling's the naked truth.

English proverb

It is terribly amusing how many
different climates of feeling one
can go through in one day.

Anne Morrow Lindbergh (b. 1906)
American writer and aviator

The greatest happiness is to transform one's feelings into actions.

Be happy. It's one way of being wise.

Colette [Sidonie-Gabrielle] (1873–1954)
French writer

Happiness depends more on how life strikes you than on what happens.

Andy Rooney (b. 1919)
American commentator and writer

You cannot make yourself feel something you do not feel, but you can make yourself do right in spite of your feelings.

PEARL S. BUCK (1892–1973)
AMERICAN WRITER

Half our mistakes in life arise from feeling where we ought

to think, and thinking where we ought to feel.

John Churton Collins (1848–1908)
English literary critic

*F*eelings are untidy.

Esther Hautzig (b. 1930)
Polish writer

It is the hardest thing in the world to put feeling, and deep feeling, into words.

JACK LONDON (1876–1916)
AMERICAN WRITER

Better to be without logic than without feeling.

Charlotte Brontë (1816–1855)
English poet and writer

Why is it that people who cannot show feeling presume that this is a strength and not a weakness?

May Sarton (1912–1985)
Belgian-born American writer

The emotions may be endless.

The more we express them, the more

we have to express.

E. M. FORSTER (1879–1970)
ENGLISH WRITER

I know now that man is capable of great deeds. But if he isn't capable of great emotion, he leaves me cold.

Albert Camus (1913–1960)
French writer

Anyone who says he is not emotional

is not getting what he should out of life.

Ezer Weizman (b. 1924)
Israeli president

There are some feelings that time cannot benumb.

GEORGE GORDON, LORD BYRON (1788–1824)
ENGLISH POET

I have a right to my anger, and I don't want anybody telling me I shouldn't be, that it's not nice to be, and that something's wrong with me because I get angry.

Maxine Waters (b. 1938)
American politician

The anger of lovers renews the strength of love.

Publilius Syrus
1st-century B.C. Latin writer

Nobody can teach you how to sing the blues, you have to feel the blues.

ERNESTINE ANDERSON (B. 1928)
AMERICAN JAZZ SINGER

Guilt is an emotion that has periodically served me well.

Barbara E. Mraz (b. 1944)
American cleric and teacher

There is nothing in the world so monstrously vast as our indifference.

For all your ills I give you laughter.

FRANÇOIS RABELAIS (C.1483–1553)
FRENCH SCHOLAR, WRITER, AND HUMANIST

I quickly laugh at everything for fear of having to cry.

Pierre-Augustin de Beaumarchais (1732–1799)
French playwright

*H*umor has in it a liberating element. But it also has something fine and

elevating. . . . What is fine about it is the triumph of . . . the ego's

victorious assertion of its own invulnerability.

SIGMUND FREUD (1856–1939)
AUSTRIAN PSYCHOANALYST

Love is not only something you feel. It is something you do.

David Wilkerson (b. 1931)
American writer

To love means to embrace and at the same time to withstand many
many endings, and many many beginnings—all in the same relationship.

Clarissa Pinkola Estés (b. 1943)
American psychologist and writer

A lost love is like a toothache. It'll hurt you

and it'll hurt you so much you'll finally get

rid of it. You'll miss it but you'll feel better.

DUKE ELLINGTON (1899–1974)
AMERICAN JAZZ MUSICIAN

The trust that we put in ourselves makes us feel trust in others.

François de La Rochefoucauld (1613–1680)
French writer and moralist

*A*ppreciation comes
from the senses, but gratitude
comes from the soul.

Kathryn Major
20th-century American writer

A single kind word keeps one warm for three winters.

I find ecstasy in living; the mere sense of living is joy enough.

Emily Dickinson (1830–1886)
American poet

. . . weeping may endure for a night, but joy cometh in the morning.

Psalm 30:5

*J*oy and openness come from our own contented heart.

SIDDHĀRTHA GAUTAMA [THE BUDDHA] (C. 563–483 B.C.)
PRINCE OF THE ŚĀYKAS AND FOUNDER OF BUDDHISM

Grief can take care of itself; but to get the full value of a joy you must have someone to divide it with.

Mark Twain (1835–1910)
American writer

Joy leads us to wisdom because it connects
us to all we are—our mind, heart, and spirit.

Charlotte Davis Kasl
20th-century American psychologist